Austin Brooks

OPRAH WINFREY: A RAGS TO RICHES STORY

How to Overcome Obstacles and Achieve Financial Success

Learn how Oprah Winfrey went from the shadows to the spotlight, overcoming extreme poverty to become one of today's most famous and wealthiest women.

Published by UNIBOOKS

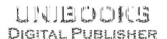

TABLE OF CONTENTS

INTRODUCTION

Oprah Winfrey is one-of-a-kind. When we hear her name, we're likely to think immediately of her incredibly famous talk show, which ran for an amazing 25 seasons, from 1986 to 2011. However, she's certainly much more than an entertainer, and the success she's seen in all areas of her life are testament to that.

Oprah grew up in a less-than-ideal environment, but was able to not only overcome her hardships, but also turn them into inspiration for her future. From the early start she had with her talk show to her ever-growing career in writing, film and television, Oprah always showed an innate ability to turn her personal reality into a way to help others, channeling her experiences into various forms of self-expression.

How much do we know about the woman behind the famous name though? In this book, we'll get a closer look at the life of one of the world's biggest stars and how she made it all happen. How did she overcome extreme poverty and turn her life into a financial success story? Learn from her strategies and create your own financial victories.

1. A BEGINNING FULL OF OBSTACLES

Oprah Winfrey is a household name today. Her talk show, as well as her other activities in the entertainment industry, have led to an incredible amount of fame and astounding economic success. It wasn't always like this for the media mogul however, and these are the aspects of Oprah's life that aren't spoken of quite as frequently, even though they played a huge role in creating her success.

The entertainer and philanthropist spent her childhood and adolescence in meager circumstances, surrounded by poverty, violence and abuse. Despite these difficulties, Oprah was able to find the path to success because of her challenges, and not in spite of them - and this could be said to be the key to her success in the long term.

Over the years, she's used her difficult life experiences as a way to reach others dealing with hardships and make a difference in the world. Every part of Oprah's life, both personal and not, shows how she turned the negative into positive, cultivating personal growth every step of the way.

1.1 Born Into a Life of Poverty

Oprah Gail Winfrey was born in Kosciusko, Mississippi, on January 29th, 1954. Named Orpah after a biblical figure, the mispronunciations that her name initially caused led her to be called Oprah by her peers, a name which eventually stuck. She was born to an unwed teenage mother who worked as a housemaid and was later sent to live with her maternal grandmother, Hattie May Lee, in less-than-ideal conditions.

The poverty which the family faced was astounding: her grandmother was so poor that Oprah often had to wear dresses made of potato sacks. She has spoken on numerous occasions about having pet cockroaches and befriending other animals that roamed the land. Her toys included a ragdoll made from a corn cob that had been dried out. When one thinks of childhood, these certainly aren't the images that should come to mind. Those precious years that one hopes to be filled with love, nurturing and happy memories were instead overflowing with difficulties and traumatizing events for the young Oprah.

Another important thing to keep in mind is that when Oprah was born in that small Mississippi town in the 1950's, civil rights had not yet swept the nation, and the rural South was a dangerous place for African Americans. Fear, hate and crime were part of daily life in those areas, and all of these factors hit close to home for a very long time. What we end up with, then, is a young and vulnerable girl who grew up in a tough, poor area and who was unable to rely on the usual comforts of home to serve as a safe house from what awaited her on the streets.

Despite all of this, there were some positive instances that would begin to steer that young girl towards a successful future. For example, Oprah learned to read at an early age, having been taught by her grandmother. Despite her mother's absence, her grandmother proved to be somewhat of a good influence on her, although she did repeatedly scold and hit the young Oprah when she misbehaved. Oprah showed a knack for memorizing and reciting bible verses, for which she was nicknamed "The Preacher."

The ability which she would later come to nourish in her professional life was certainly present from an early age. Needless to say, this would be echoed later on, when she would in fact begin to speak professionally in public and reach out to others with words of wisdom, encouragement and assistance - the very words that she needed most during those early years of her life.

1.2 A Traumatizing Adolescence

Unfortunately, Oprah's hardships didn't end with her early childhood. After years of living with her grandmother, she moved to Milwaukee, Wisconsin with her mother, Vernita Lee. Since her mother worked such long and tedious hours, she was less supportive and less helpful towards Oprah than her grandmother had been in Mississippi. During this time, Oprah's mother gave birth to a second child, which put an added strain on the family's financial situation, already incredibly tight.

Raising both girls also proved to be nearly impossible for their mother, a reason for which Oprah was sent to live temporarily with her father, Vernon Winfrey, in Nashville, Tennessee. At this time, her mother gave birth to a third daughter and would later come to give birth to Oprah's brother, Jeffrey. Jeffrey would later die of AIDS-related causes in 1989, while Oprah's sister Patricia died from a cocaine addiction in 2003. Oprah only learned that she had a second half-sister in 2010 - a startling, bittersweet revelation.

The time period during which Oprah stayed with her father marked some of the most difficult and traumatizing events for Oprah. When she was living with Vernon, Oprah was abused by a number of different men. She has mentioned on her talk show as well as in other instances that she was sexually molested by an uncle, a family friend and a cousin. She was also abused by men in her mother's circle during different periods of her life.

The sexual and physical abuse started when she was just 9 years old, and when she finally worked up the courage to speak out about it in her early twenties, her family reacted in disbelief and refused to support her or believe what she was telling them. This was another blow to the young Oprah, but it also goes to show how wonderful it is that she would go on to serve as a listener to so many people later on, helping in turn to lessen, if not solve, their problems.

Oprah passed through the hallways of a couple of high schools in her teenage years before moving on to college. She had become pregnant at age 13, but her baby was premature and died shortly after birth. She was sent by her mother to an affluent high school where she felt out of touch with the reality of her peers, most of whom were wealthy and white. She began to steal from her family in order to try and fit in on an economic level and to spend time with older students, which worried and frustrated her mother, who ultimately sent her back to her father. Oprah would not return to live with Vernita after this incident, and would remain with Vernon until her career began to take off.

Luckily enough for Oprah, her father was more strict than her mother was and pushed her academically when she enrolled at East Nashville High School. She started to do well in school and also began delving in different extracurricular activities, including drama and speech.

She went on to win an oratory contest, which led to her securing a scholarship to Tennessee State University. At this point, her penchant for the media and for oratory was starting to blossom fully and would begin to attract the attention of various outlets. Furthermore, it would catapult her to the fame that was just around the corner.

1.3 The Light at the End of the Tunnel

The turning point in Oprah's academic life proved to be her saving grace. Local black media radio station WVOL hired her, and she later moved on to local television to cover the news. She also began to dabble in interview programs and to co-anchor certain segments of the news on TV, which she'd shown a knack for early on in her life. However, Oprah proved too sentimental for journalism.

The emotional detachment required by most journalism outlets was unfathomable to the young woman who so longed to make a connection with others, to share her story, to lend a hand. This was not, however, a total setback: what could be called a difficulty in journalistic duties led to her brilliance as a host.

Being able to openly laugh, cry, show emotion onstage - that was what Oprah had been longing for. The chance to connect with the people who attended her show would serve as both an outlet for her guests and herself. In 1983, Oprah hosted Chicago's *AM Chicago* show on WLS-TV. In an incredibly short period of time, Oprah brought the ratings up from unsettlingly low. In 1986, *The Oprah Winfrey Show* was born, thanks to the generous helping hand of critic Roger Ebert, who noticed Oprah's talent at once and gave her a shot at proving just how good she really was. And that is what she did.

It may seem an unnecessarily obvious declaration, but in those days working conditions were not the same as today: Oprah rose to fame in a professional setting almost entirely dominated by white males. This is an incredible feat when we remember her beginnings, marked by poverty and explicit racism. Her personality and emotional accessibility would prove to be two of the strong points which would make her audiences tune in so religiously, so loyally, in the future.

The Oprah Winfrey Show began to go where no other show had gone before, to cover issues and topics that were often times not mentioned on national television. Oprah could talk about anything from politics to science to tourism to spirituality: it all worked. Television ended up being the light at the end of the tunnel for the young woman from rural Mississippi, the one place where she could finally shine through the help she'd come to offer her ever-growing audience. And there was no turning back.

This isn't one of those stories about a person born into a life of privilege and wealth. Oprah had to build the life she wanted almost literally from scratch. If you're struggling with something in your professional or personal life, it's important to take the time to step back and distance yourself from the situation in order to properly analyze it.

Ask yourself whether the issue is as big as you think it is: blowing things out of proportion often lessens our ability to deal with the problems at hand. Define the problems you're facing and think about the things you can do to alleviate them or solve them altogether, especially if these issues are holding you back in some way, keeping you from moving forward.

Oprah was able to leave behind poverty, racism and discrimination as well as a traumatizing series of childhood events in order to continue her path to success. You can too: focus on the ultimate end, the final goal in your mind in order to lessen the burden of the means which are, ultimately, temporary.

As Oprah once said, "the biggest adventure you can ever take is to live the life of your dreams."

2. FROM NO BUSINESS TO SHOW BUSINESS: HER FIRST TV APPEARANCES

As we've come to see, Oprah rose to success quite rapidly once she was able to show her talent as an interviewer on television. She quickly showed the world that she was relatable, kind, generous, and not afraid to show her true colors, however faded these may have been.

The contrast between her success - both professional and financial at this point - and her indisputably humble past is astounding. Oprah went from playing with corn cob dolls she'd fashion herself to having people dedicated around the clock to her wellbeing, health and aesthetics. It was quite the 180 turn. To better understand just how Oprah began to climb her way to the top, it's important to look at the beginnings of her professional days in deeper detail.

2.1 Part-time News

When Oprah started her television career, she was just a sophomore in college. The Nashville CBS affiliate had offered her a job twice already before doing so a third time, when Oprah finally said yes - she had turned them down twice. However, thanks to the influence of both her teachers and her father, she was able to continue to succeed and grow both academically and professionally. It wasn't too long ago, after all, that Oprah had been experiencing serious difficulties both within her family and within her school environment. The fact that she was able to leave this behind and begin constructing her personal and professional growth is a laudable feat.

The appearance of the Nashville CBS affiliate in Oprah's life led to one of her first major milestones, as she was the first African American female co-anchor on the evening news. After she graduated from college, she moved on to Baltimore, Maryland, where she was hired to do the local news updates on *Good Morning America* and then moved on to a talk show called *Baltimore Is Talking*, with co-host Richard Sher.

She was finally hired by the American Broadcasting Company's Chicago affiliate - her ratings had been consistently higher than Phil Donahue's, a well-known program host, and thus attracted the interest of several news stations and personalities. Her talent was undeniable.

As a result, Oprah moved to Chicago, where she would finally cement her knack for carrying out the tasks of a talk show host: she changed the topics on *A.M. Chicago* to focus on more controversial, debatable topics. The ratings skyrocketed. Within a month, the program's ratings were even with those of Donahue's program. Within a few months' time, they were even higher.

The show, renamed *The Oprah Winfrey Show*, was such a success that its running time was expanded to an hour. The program itself was syndicated, airing on a large number of stations and channels, and she began to make more and more money, which culminated in her buying the rights from ABC and placing it under her new production company, HARPO Studios.

2.2 A Taste of Success

Oprah's charisma certainly played a role in her success, as she was seen as relatable, kind and caring on television. The way she interacted with the people on the show made them want to open up and share their stories, often holding little back from their host. She took her job as a way to reach out to others and educate people, helping them with their troubles.

All of these factors led to the program growing more and more popular, which of course led to financial gains for Oprah, which would become huge over time. It seemed that ever since she gained control of *The Oprah Winfrey Show*, she had become unstoppable. This also led to her being noticed by film producers and actors, which would open up a new door for Oprah: film. We'll look into this aspect of her life in a later chapter. Notice though: Once Oprah began rising to fame, she never looked back.

Oprah is now one of the wealthiest and best paid women in the United States. Initially, there weren't many things in her life which could be grouped under the umbrella of "success." Once she began to take off, however, her flight path to the top was unstoppable.

2.3 The Consolidation of the Oprah Winfrey Show

The Oprah Winfrey Show took off due to the topics prioritized by its new host, as well as due to Oprah's personality and obvious natural ability to connect with both viewers and guests. At the time, talk shows were often seen as trashy or less serious programs, with many of the topics found interesting by a more marginalized sector of the United States' population.

It was often difficult for viewers to connect with what they saw on the screen, which had a direct result in those programs' ratings as well as in how their viewer population was comprised. In this sense, the effect that Oprah and her new show had on television and talk shows can be considered revolutionary, having had a profound effect on what comes to mind when one hears the term talk show.

Oprah initially changed the topics, as was previously mentioned, that were to be discussed onstage. This initially had negative results, and ratings began to drop. However, shortly after, the ratings would go right back up again as viewers began to notice Oprah's respect and genuine concern towards everyone around her. The issues that were brought up on the program also began to interest wider audiences, and more and more people began to tune in to what would become a staple of talk show television. By September of 1986, the program was being broadcast in 138 cities and towns, which was expected to bring in over $120 million in revenue.

If you seem stuck professionally or feel like you're not advancing, ask yourself why you think that may be. It's often easy to place the blame on others and feel like we deserve something because we've been sticking it out for a while or because we've been doing very well for some time. However, success is more than just positive reinforcement being handed to you, even if it is well-deserved.

You have to pave your own path to success, and this will certainly mean starting from the bottom in many cases, as well as overcoming difficult situations along the way. You may meet people who stifle you or who are negative influences on your life, whether it be professional or personal. Surround yourself with inspirational people and learn to differentiate the people who will help and inspire you from those who will hold you back or simply want something from you.

"Surround yourself only with people who are going to lift you higher." - Oprah Winfrey

3. THE OPRAH WINFREY SHOW AND HARPO STUDIOS: A SUCCESS STORY

The Oprah Winfrey Show had become a part of HARPO Studios, which had purchased the rights to the program once it began to show huge signs of success. HARPO Studios, in turn, also became a successful business endeavor for Oprah and grew significantly over the years alongside the show itself. It's now famous and very wealthy leader would be responsible for even more.

3.1 The Interviews That Made It Happen

During her time as host of *The Oprah Winfrey Show*, Oprah interviewed countless amazing personalities, some of them famous, some of them not. Naming them all and going into the details that made each of those interviews special would be extremely time consuming, if not impossibly daunting.

To get an idea of the full impact of these interviews, however, we can take a look at those which are considered milestones for both the program itself and its host. These are the interviews which cemented the show's reputation, the ones that people kept talking about long after the television was turned off.

The very first episode featured was called "How to Marry the Man of Your Dreams," but those kinds of topics would soon be left behind. Oprah would go on

21

to interview both everyday people with a variety of issues and stories to tell, as well as A-list celebrities that would lead to some serious post-show buzz. One of the early examples of a memorable interview is from the 1980's, when Mike Sisco was interviewed. Sisco was a gay man suffering from AIDS; he spoke of his trials as well as the issues raised when he swam in a public pool, causing an uproar among the public. The AIDS epidemic had just begun and not much was yet known about it.

Because of this, people were often treated with horrific discrimination. It was typical of Oprah to bring a man who had been at the forefront of such discrimination on to her show. Another memorable interview from around the same time period was the Truddi Chase episode.

Chase was a woman who had suffered such traumatizing abuse in her early childhood and through her early adolescence that her psyche had split itself into 92 distinct personalities - unheard of before in Multiple Personality Disorder or Dissociative Identity Disorder.

Over the years, we've also witnessed some incredibly unforgettable celebrity interviews. In 1993, Michael Jackson was interviewed by Oprah. He was already beginning to show signs of erratic behavior and overall strangeness, and rarely granted interviews. He granted her a free-for-all questioning session in which Oprah headed over to the Neverland Ranch and proceeded to speak with Michael Jackson for what would become one of her most-watched episodes. Over 100 million people tuned in. Ellen DeGeneres came out on her program. In 2005, Tom Cruise went on the show and began jumping on Oprah's couch in a display of extreme emotion which would certainly never be forgotten. Oprah's reactions were also priceless.

Rihanna went on to discuss her relationship with Chris Brown, who had been physically abusive towards the well-known singer. The host would even confront several well-known personalities amidst controversy, such as author James Frey, whose memoir about drug abuse was actually shown to have been fabricated. Having been recommended by Oprah for her extremely popular book club, these allegations proved too much for the host: she had to have him on her show to talk about what had happened.

Angering Oprah Winfrey is certainly not on anybody's to-do list. Actors, singers, writers, politicians, people who were all over the news, child personalities: they all sat on her couch and spoke with the queen of talk show television. Her best friend Gayle, her famous friends, they were all a part of what would become television history. Over time, even the President of the United States and his wife Michelle Obama would grace the show with their presence.

As we can see through all of these examples, Oprah didn't limit her interviews whatsoever. She brought the good and the bad, the beautiful and the ugly. She did funny episodes, but she also did some of the most heart-wrenching. She talked about some of the best things that can happen to a person, putting smiles on everyone's faces, but she also brought serious, difficult topics such as physical and sexual abuse to light.

Poverty, disease, drug abuse, family drama - they all made the cut, and Oprah was there every step of the way to ensure that each episode was perfect and to offer her larger-than-life grain of salt to the show: her experiences were priceless themselves, and her empathy unquestionable. Never forgetting her past difficulties, she made them a part of every episode, in a more or less obvious manner. Mirroring herself in those she spoke with was part of her magic, and a talent and capability that not many more people have been able to demonstrate.

3.2 HARPO Studios, Controversies and More

A major part of Oprah's business life and success is HARPO Studios. HARPO is Oprah spelled backwards, and she founded the company in 1986. It is the sole subsidiary of her media and entertainment company, Harpo Inc. Due to the fact that Oprah founded HARPO Studios so early on in her career, it has become an inextricable part of her television life and success. Due to the show having ended in 2011, there wasn't much left for the studio itself, although it wasn't until quite recently that the media mogul decided that she would relocate to California.

Unfortunately for its staff, layoffs were a part of this relocating process and serious downsizing was inevitable. Oprah announced in March 2015 that she would be laying off the majority of HARPO employees, to which she often referred to as the greatest team in television. This was, of course, quite the change for the production company, which had over 12,000 employees at its peak in 2012. The shows Dr. Phil, Rachel Ray and Dr. Oz were also produced at the studios. However, after *The Oprah Winfrey Show* ended in 2011, there really wasn't any need for the Chicago studio space, and Oprah decided to relocate operations to California and shut the Chicago base down.

Despite obvious fame and success, the studio did find itself in a few sticky situations over the years. In fact, it was rather early on that Oprah had her first taste of backlash. After speaking about Mad Cow Disease on her program, the media queen said that fear of the disease had stopped her from eating even one more burger. This did not go over well with Texas cattle ranchers, who promptly sued her for defamation. In 2008, Winfrey had declined to invite Sarah Palin to her program until after the elections, which sparked some serious backlash.

Over the years, the studio also had to deal with the FCC (due to supposedly explicit content on certain episodes), politicians, and angry viewers in general (mostly parents whose children perhaps tuned in to the program at some point during the day). It is, of course, an impossible feat to keep everybody happy at the same time, and looking at the general picture of the program and the history of HARPO Studios, we can conclude that its long history doesn't look too shabby. Oprah ended the show, which would subsequently lead to the end of HARPO Studios, in an extremely positive light.

3.3 The End of an Era

It was in 2009 that Oprah officially announced the end of her show. She let her viewers know 18 months beforehand that she thought 25 years was the perfect running time for her and the show, and that she was forever grateful for her viewers and the support they had provided over the years. The season premiere of the show's last season was Monday, September 13th, 2010. Winfrey brought John Travolta onstage and announced to their 300 audience members that they'd be accompanying her to Australia and the Sydney Opera House to film episodes there.

Travolta would be the pilot. The episode also included flashbacks and fans' memories and experiences over the years with the show. It was an emotional time for all, one that would mark television history and that also provided a taste of what was to come during that season, which was certainly going to be spectacular.

On April 14th, 2011, the 30-day countdown to the final episode began. Emotions were running high, and each show up until the last one featured notable personalities thanking Oprah for her work. In May 2011, Barack Obama and Michelle Obama were featured on the program, during which Oprah was also thanked for her work and told that she connected better than anyone they knew with the American audience.

Oprah was able to turn her trauma and drama into a way to help others, primarily through her show and the interviews which would cement her fame. Often times, it may feel like our issues are going to weigh us down permanently. However, in order to grow as a person and continue moving forward on the long path of our lives, we need to not look back on our pasts with nostalgia, fear or hate and instead use negative instances to ask ourselves a series of questions:

- What did I learn from these events?
- How did I feel about them at the time? How do I feel about them now?
- What would I say to myself in that situation if I could go back in time and speak to the past me?
- How can I use this advice to help others or turn these negative experiences into something positive in the present?

Through her interviews, of which there were many with both very famous people and run of the mill citizens of the world, Oprah gave herself and others a voice.

"Breathe. Let go. And remind yourself that this very moment is the only one you know you have for sure." - Oprah Winfrey

4. NOT JUST TELEVISION: A LOOK INSIDE OPRAH'S WRITING AND FILM WORK

It's easy to think of *The Oprah Winfrey Show* as the primary source of Oprah's fame over the years. After all, it certainly was the most popular of all her endeavors and remained successful throughout its lengthy run. However, as we've touched upon beforehand, the program wasn't the only thing keeping Oprah busy during the day. She had a number of other projects going on simultaneously, and despite their not being completely in the spotlight all of the time, they were certainly important and most of them ended up doing quite well.

The traits that helped Oprah garner success on her program were also applied to her other tasks, and she is a prime example of how to successfully multitask professionally, letting her thirst for success leak over into other areas, both personal and professional. You'll hopefully gain the knowledge to apply these ideas and tactics in your own life.

4.1 Online Work and Radio

Out of all of the projects important to Oprah, her online work was at the top. It's important to keep in mind that when *The Oprah Winfrey Show* aired, the internet didn't exist. For the majority of the people reading this, that's a mind blowing thing to grasp because our present lives so wholly depend on the

29

internet for the majority of things we do throughout the day. Oprah's program aired in the 80's and ended in 2011, so it saw many a change in society, culture, politics and much more over its long, long run. The internet and its influence was one of them, and a very important one at that. True to her nature, when the internet began to take off, Oprah began taking advantage of it in order to make sure it could be useful to her entertainment projects. It certainly was.

First of all, Oprah.com became a staple for the program and its host since it provided audiences all over the world with easy access to video clips, stories, forums and much more. It also allowed people to share their own stories and also participate in a huge number of sweepstakes, contests, etc., which could put them in touch with the star herself or bring them closer to making their own dreams come true.

The website included recommendations for reading material, shows to watch, apps to download - everything you could think of. In a way, it was the perfect and most important way to accompany *The Oprah Winfrey Show* on a non-televised platform, and the stats have shown that traffic held steady over time.

Today, due to the show having been off the air for several years now, the site isn't as popular, which isn't a surprise. However, back when Oprah was at the height of her success and the internet was showing its true colors in terms of how people could connect with each other and stay connected, it proved to be a gigantic success. Finally, viewers could also tune in to the show online, which was possibly the most exciting aspect of the website.

In addition to her online ventures, Oprah also dabbled in radio. Oprah Radio went on the air in 2006, hosted by the radio division from HARPO Productions. Much like *The Oprah Winfrey Show* itself, it included regular programming that focused on a wide variety of topics such as current events, politics, health and fitness, etc. Some of the most notable personalities that went on the radio show included Oprah's best friend, Gayle King, along with Dr. Oz, Bob Greene and Nate Berkus.

4.2 Writing: O, The Oprah Magazine, and more

As if television and radio weren't enough, Oprah spearheaded a number of written projects as well. Most importantly, perhaps, was *O, The Oprah Magazine*. Founded by Oprah, the monthly magazine was first published in the year 2000. It averaged almost three million copies, most by subscription, and its main target was women. One of its notable traits is that Oprah appears on the cover every month, with only a few shared covers having appeared over its history.

Just like her television talk show, the magazine also proved to be influential in a variety of areas including the culinary and entertainment industries, not to mention the influence that the magazine itself had on women's magazines in general.

In the same way that *The Oprah Winfrey Show* had an effect on daytime television, so did *O, The Oprah Magazine* influence these types of publications. The common element was, of course, the star responsible for it all. Luckily for readers, the magazine was made available digitally for cell phones and tablets via app stores, and readers could subscribe just like they did with the paper version.

Fans of Oprah's written work will be happy to know that the multifaceted, do-it-all superstar is penning a memoir which is set to appear at some time in 2017.

4.3 Film Work

Last but not least, Oprah was also a part of the movie industry. The most notorious of all the movies she was in is probably *The Color Purple*, from 1985. Oprah played Sofia in the film, which was directed by Steven Spielberg. This information alone is enough to give us a hint of Oprah's popularity even as long ago as 30 years ago.

It also goes to show that there was an interest early on in both film and literature, with the movie being based on the novel by Alice Walker, also called *The Color Purple*. As we all now know, Oprah led an extremely popular and successful book club - so popular, in fact, that being featured on the host's list was practically a guarantee of success in terms of sales and fandom for the featured book.

The movie's plot also reflects some of Oprah's own personal trials and tribulations, dealing with physical and sexual abuse and the manners in which the young woman involved overcomes different traumatizing events in her life.

Overall, it's been said to be a relatively accurate depiction of these issues as well as the African American characters who are the protagonists.. The movie also went on to become a Broadway musical in 2005 due to its popularity and overall success, with Oprah listed as a producer in the production.

Another movie based on a novel which Oprah produced and subsequently starred in was 1998's *Beloved*. This film also dealt with African Americans and their history, with slavery as the main topic. Oprah prepared thoroughly for the role, although the film itself didn't fare too well at the box office. In 2005, Zora Neale Hurston's 1937 novel *Their Eyes Were Watching God* was released with Halle Berry as the lead female. There are countless other examples of Oprah's movie career, which even included stints in animated films: she was the voice of Gussie the Goose in the 2006 version of *Charlotte's Web*.

Oprah didn't just stop at television, but instead went on to cultivate her love of entertainment through various other media outlets. Radio, writing, film - you name it, she did it. If you have a passion for something, don't let anything stifle it. Continue to think about all of the ways you can grow as a person and let your passion grow as well. Oprah could have stopped at any time, as she was certainly riddled by fear and insecurities, especially when she was younger.

However, she certainly did no such thing, instead choosing to power through the difficulties and use the lows in her life as inspiration and a window into others' personal issues. Instead of being afraid of what people might say or what may happen to her professionally, she did her own thing and created a world of her own so powerful that the term "Oprahfication" has been coined to describe it. Yes, that's right: her very own word in the English language.

"I believe that one of life's greatest risks is never daring to risk." - Oprah Winfrey

5. SUCCESSFUL CAREER, GARGANTUAN FORTUNE

Even if you didn't know much about Oprah before reading about her life, it's not hard to believe that she's not doing too shabby financially. She has remained an almost ubiquitous presence over the past three decades and it's almost impossible to have missed her on magazines, television, movies or the internet. She is, for all intents and purposes, a superstar.

Her successful career has led to an enormous financial fortune that leaves many other wealthy personages in the dust. What's even more amazing is comparing Oprah's life today to the one she led as a child and teenager: she's come a long way, and not just economically speaking.

5.1 A Far Cry from Rural Poverty

Oprah's net worth today is 3 billion dollars. Let that sink in for a moment as we ponder where that fortune came from and what it means. She's a self-made billionaire, which is an incredible feat considering the wonderful, generous work she's done and the fact that she didn't exactly have much help along the way.

Oprah is also featured on a few Forbes' lists: she's #5 on America's Self-Made Women list, #12 on Power Women and #64 on Powerful People, not to mention that her name is also on the lists of both American and

World Billionaires. She was on the highest-paid celebrity list four years in a row, from 2008 to 2012. Because of her wealth, she is now one of the world's richest African Americans, as well as one of the most influential.

Due to her wealth, Oprah has been able to support the careers of many other people throughout the years. Among the most notable are Dr. Phil, Rachel Ray, Dr. Oz, and her own best friend Gayle King. A little bit of investment from Oprah, or a tiny amount of her touting a product, a book or a show, makes a world of difference.

This is especially evident when we take a look at her famous book club: a mention from Oprah means immediate and huge sales. In fact, USA Today has described Oprah as "America's most popular reader." Finally, and just in case it isn't quite clear yet, Oprah's net worth tops the GDP of several countries, being large enough to fund her own cable TV network for two more decades completely out of pocket. Not bad for the world's first ever female African American billionaire.

5.2 Philanthropic Interests

Our hats are off to Oprah when it comes to her handling of her fortune: she doesn't just hold on tight; she shares, invests and develops a wide range of programs to fund everything from education to entertainment to athletics. There is a lot of generosity behind the wealth. Philanthropy has always been a top priority for Oprah, and she was named among America's 50 most generous people in 2004. One of the best examples of this generosity is her Oprah's Angel Network, which she created in 1998. The wonderful thing about this organization is that it supported a wide range of charities, not focusing on just one specific issue or problem.

It raised over $80,000,000 and all administrative costs were covered by Oprah out of pocket, which meant keeping 100% of donations geared towards charitable causes. After the end of her program having been announced in 2010, the charity was shut down. As further evidence of her generosity, in 2005, after Hurricane Katrina, Oprah created a registry which raised over $11,000,000.

Outside of the United States, Oprah created the Oprah Winfrey Leadership Academy for Girls in South Africa. The school opened in 2007 and focused on disadvantaged young girls from South Africa, allowing them to grow academically and, as a result, personally, in luxurious surroundings. World leaders from Bill Clinton to Nelson Mandela have praised the institution, with the latter saying that he thought it extremely laudable that Oprah had been able to overcome her personal hardships and go on to help others in magnificent ways.

5.3 Rankings

As we've come to see, Oprah is one powerful and amazing woman. News outlets like CNN and Time have referred to her as possibly the world's most influential. In fact, *TIME* named her one of the most influential people from 2004 to 2011, and she is the only person in the world to have appeared on that list so many times. Her success and influence is also important due to the fact that she is both African American and a woman.

She is undoubtedly an influential figure, but the fact that she carries with her the weight of two minorities is also extremely noteworthy. She has achieved the success that many only dream of, and the people who do in fact go on to succeed so greatly in their lifetimes are not usually burdened with past traumas as Oprah is, nor do they carry the social stigma that inevitably comes with being a female African American in a professional environment dominated by white men.

The Greatest American poll from 2005 named Oprah the greatest American woman. She has stayed at the top of a long list of rankings which range from those that measure wealth, popularity, influence, etc. Although her numbers have varied over time, they have stayed high overall. When we take a look at the work she's done, the highs and lows from her life, it's truly marvelous and praiseworthy. She is an example to all woman, and to all people, who have gone through difficult moments and believed that they may never reach the top or live out their dreams. Everything is possible, and not just in monetary terms: one can go on to find love and success in all walks of life if the focus is kept on the future, on one's goals and what are considered to each person to be the most important things in life.

One of the most important things we can learn from Oprah is how to deal with such a large amount of fame and fortune. Far from being selfish, Oprah has given back in huge amounts to the community, both local and not. She herself has said that the reason she's been so financially successful has to do with her focus - and it's never been about the money. Now that she has it, and plenty of it at that, she makes sure to invest. Although it's unlikely that your financial situation will ever reach the status of the world's wealthiest African American woman, you can still ask yourself how to help others with what you do have.

Every gesture counts, no matter how small it may seem to you. Keeping the positive energy flowing will bring results in the end, as the most important thing in life is to keep your head up and help others do the same.

"Turn your wounds into wisdom." - Oprah Winfrey

6. PERSONAL LIFE, PERSONAL GAINS

As we've already mentioned, Oprah's gains haven't just been financial. Although these are noteworthy for reason's we've touched upon, it's also equally important to mention and keep in mind the personal gains that Oprah has acquired over time. All of the money in the world wouldn't be enough for anybody if they didn't feel well spiritually, emotionally, physically. This truth is no different for Oprah: she's learned to cultivate strong personal bonds, adding friendships and relationships that would leave a mark on her life's path.

6.1 Stedman and Gayle

Perhaps the best-known people who are always side-by-side with Oprah are her partner, Stedman Graham, and her best friend, Gayle King. Oprah and Stedman have been in a relationship since the 1980's, and he has been a staple in her life ever since. Although they were originally going to be married, they later decided that they would rather put emphasis on a spiritual union.

Stedman is such a special person for Oprah that he even appeared with her on a cover of *O, The Oprah Magazine* - only a handful of people have accompanied the star on the cover since the publication first came out. Oprah and Stedman have maintained a very private relationship as well and have remained out of the spotlight, marking a difference from the usual celebrity-couple mania that we see in the papers or on TV.

This is, perhaps, one of the main reasons why their love has triumphed over the years. There is quite literally a lack of information, photos, etc. about Oprah and Stedman on the internet or in magazines. Every once in a while, a bit of information about the couple would be shared by Oprah herself, or a picture would be published with Oprah's prior consent. Stedman has also been on television with the superstar. These have all been instances that were preapproved by both Oprah and Stedman, not paparazzi-related publications.

Equally important is Oprah's lifelong best friend, Gayle King. Gayle and Oprah have been friends since their early twenties, and Oprah has supported her professionally over the years, leading to King having a talk show of her own as well as being editor of Oprah's magazine. Oprah's relationship with Gayle has been in the spotlight more than her relationship with Stedman, and their obvious closeness has also led to rumors that the two were involved romantically at some point. However, this has always been adamantly denied by Oprah, who has claimed that she is someone who has put it all out there for her viewers and the world, and would never be ashamed of being gay.

Her bond with her best female friend is something that our culture doesn't really have words for, she says, and so people often try and explain it through sexuality. The rumors have never stopped the two from keeping their friendship strong and in the public eye, with articles, pictures and television programs dedicated to one of the two women, or both, popping up at some point or another over time.

Surrounding yourself with people who are going to help you succeed is vital to your well-being. It's key to filter out the individuals who are only looking to benefit themselves, or who seem to be focused on toxicity and negativity. After all, it's your road to the top that you're paving - it's important to build a small but positive circle of people who will accompany you no matter what.

"Surround yourself with only people who are going to lift you higher." - Oprah Winfrey

6.2 Interests and Endorsements
Despite being a billionaire and a superstar known all over the world, Oprah Winfrey is, at the end of the day, a woman and a human being just like any of us. She has hobbies, interests and preferences with regards to food, entertainment and more just like anybody else would. She loves food, movies and literature, and has cited *To Kill A Mockingbird* by Harper Lee as her favorite novel of all time. Her biggest interest, however, is probably helping others,

making a difference in people's lives and, ultimately, in the world. She has channeled her interests in the form of organizations, charities and sporadic activities dedicated to helping people who need it the most.

Her Angel Network, her work in South Africa and the donations she's made over the years to educational facilities show that she is dedicated to helping foster academics and helping stimulate children who do not have equal opportunities or access to education. Because of her, there are hundreds of girls in South Africa with a top-tier education who would never have otherwise dreamed of living such a life.

She's also shown her interest in different topics and issues by endorsing specific products, organizations or persons over the years which, of course, skyrocketed their popularity. She publicly supported Barack Obama in the 2008 and 2012 presidential races, for example. In addition, she's backed Weight Watchers by buying shares in the company and publicly speaking about the organization as well as their healthy-living philosophy, Spanx, Amazon Kindle, and numerous other things. The better known endorsements are her favorite books, with her book club being hugely popular and sales for featured works doing extremely well after having been mentioned on Oprah's coveted list. She inarguably has a Midas touch.

6.3 Lesser Known Facts

To close our biography on Oprah, we thought it would be appropriate to name a few fun or lesser known facts about Oprah, her show and her life. Often, the focus is placed on what the media decides to talk about and there are many details which, although perhaps less important, slip through the cracks. These details, however, allow us to form a complete picture of the woman Oprah Winfrey is.

One of the things we've mentioned about Oprah is her undeniable influence. In 2003, she mentioned the We Take The Cake bakery in Florida, which hadn't been doing too well in sales lately. After the mention, the bakery's owner said that their phone rang nonstop for two weeks. Oprah has certainly turned the fate of several people, families and businesses around over the years.

She's also been very generous, both on her program and off. One of her more well-known segments is "Oprah's Favorite Things," where she showcases something she really loves and then shares it with the audience - who gets to take the item/s home or try them out for themselves. The first ever segment of her favorite things in 1997 featured her in red and white checkered pajamas, by Karen Neuburger. The most expensive famous thing she featured on her program was a Volkswagen Beetle, priced at almost $19,000 (the 2012 model given to audience members in 2010). She also once gave members iPads, which were lowered down into the crowd on angel wings. Needless to say, audience members have gotten some pretty amazing things over the years.

Other fun facts about Oprah include that she was shown to be 8% Native American after a DNA test and that she was awarded the Presidential Medal of Freedom by Barack Obama in 2013. This is the nation's highest civilian honor. She was also featured on a 1998 cover of *Vogue* magazine. She also loves animals and has several pets of her own.

CONCLUSION

Oprah Winfrey is an example for all of us. The story of her life is inspirational, if not downright amazing. Born into a life of abject poverty, she climbed out of the hole she found herself in up through her adolescent years to become one of the most successful people in the world and the wealthiest African American woman. Her talk show, magazine, radio programs, movies and written work have been incredibly successful and have helped people all over the world who found themselves in different problematic situations.

The fact that she left behind the negativity which surrounded her at one point in time in order to begin to help others is very laudable. She amassed a huge fortune, over 3 billion dollars, but was never greedy, choosing instead to donate millions of dollars, invest in the issues which were most important to her and buy a long list of items for people - whether they be people in her audience or people in need.

She has also surrounded herself with people who care about her and didn't end up using her or hurting her, although she has had experiences with that in the past. It's almost inevitable to meet people who wish to take advantage of you when you're that rich and famous, but the people she cares for most have always been there from the very beginning, and will likely be there until the end. Having had such a thirst for healthy love in her younger years, the fact that she can show herself to be so loving and nurturing to others, to her partner and her friends, is also not a fact to be overlooked. It seems that every part of Oprah's life, every little detail, holds an example, some behavior to mimic. After all, it's not every day that a dirt poor African American girl born in a place without much opportunity becomes one of the most famous women in the world. And asking ourselves what allowed Oprah to make that (albeit long) transition is the first step in applying the tools and measures which led to her one-of-a-kind success.

THE END

27033495R00029

Made in the USA
San Bernardino, CA
24 February 2019